SHOPPING

D1337392

Contents

Dee Reid

**Story illustrated by
Martin Chatterton**

Heinemann

Find out about

- Some really expensive toys

Tricky words

- what
- would
- buy
- money

Introduce these tricky words and help the reader when they come across them later!

Text starter

Some toys cost a lot of money. If you had lots of money, would you buy an Audi pedal car, or a life-size Batman Lego model? Perhaps you would buy a very expensive teddy? So what toy would you buy if you had lots of money?

What Would You Buy?

What toy would you buy
if you had lots of money?

Lots of kids would buy a car.
Would you buy a car?

This car costs £6,500.

Would you spend £6,500 on a car?

Auto Union Type C

Lots of kids would buy Lego.
Would you buy Lego?

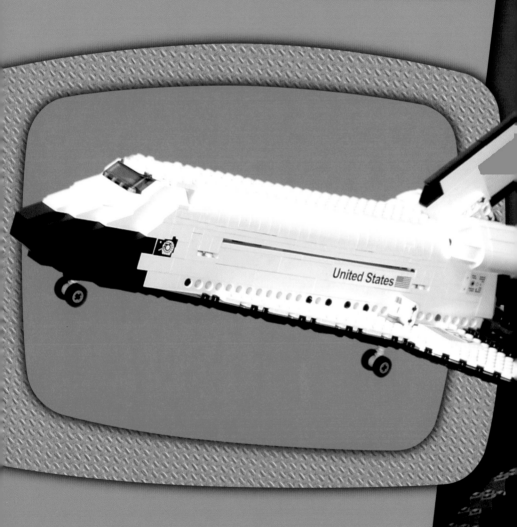

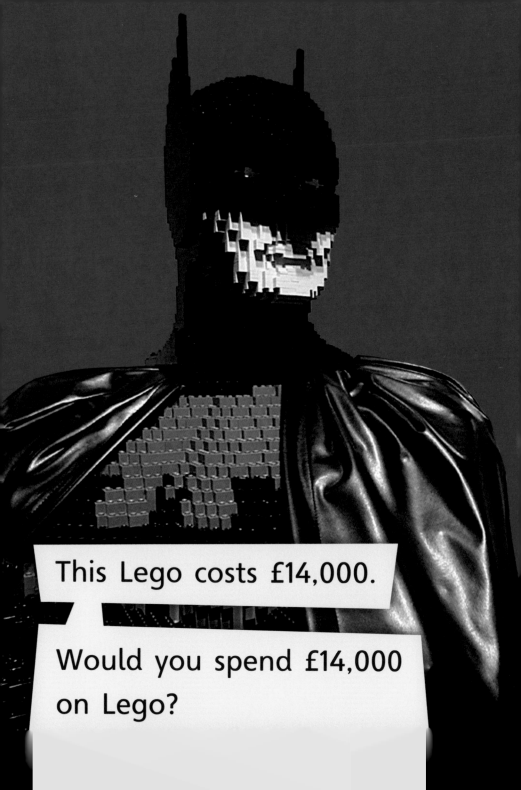

Lots of kids would buy a teddy.
Would you buy a teddy?

This teddy has eyes made of diamonds!

This teddy costs £43,000.

Would you spend £43,000 on a teddy?

So what toy would you buy
if you had lots of money?

Quiz

Text Detective

- Which toy was the most expensive?
- Do you like shopping?

Word Detective

- Phonic Focus: Final phonemes
  Page 3: Find a word ending with the phoneme 't'.
- Page 3: How many syllables (beats) are there in the word 'money'?
- Page 9: Which sentence is a question? How can you tell?

Super Speller

Read these words:

had   if

Now try to spell them!

HA! HA! HA!

Q Where can you always find money when you look for it?

A In a dictionary.

11

In this story

Silly Sid

Tricky words

- kind
- glasses
- these
- pants

Introduce these tricky words and help the reader when they come across them later!

Story starter

Silly Sid is a bit silly. One day, Silly Sid needed a new hat, so he went to the shops to get a hat.

Silly Sid Goes Shopping

"I need a new hat," said Silly Sid.

Silly Sid got a new hat.

Silly Sid put it on.

"I am silly," said Silly Sid.
"This is not the kind of hat
I need."

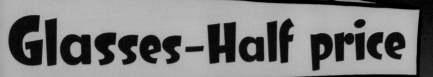

Glasses-Half price

"I need some new glasses," said Silly Sid.

Silly Sid got some glasses.

What has Silly Sid done wrong?

Silly Sid put them on.

"I am silly," said Silly Sid. "These are not the kind of glasses I need."

"I need some new pants," said Silly Sid.

Silly Sid got some new pants.

"I am not so silly," said Silly Sid.

Quiz

Text Detective

- What was wrong with the glasses Silly Sid tried on?
- Do you think Silly Sid is silly? Why?

Word Detective

- Phonic Focus: Final phonemes

  Page 18: Find a word ending with the phoneme 'd'.
- Page 17: Find a word that means 'sort'.
- Page 22: Find a word that rhymes with 'feed'.

Super Speller

Read these words:

hat   are

Now try to spell them!

HA! HA! HA!

 What's the difference between a well-dressed man and a tired dog?

One wears a suit, the other just pants.